Learning to Feel Good
and Stay Cool

Published by
MAGINATION PRESS
An Educational Publishing Foundation Book
American Psychological Association
750 First Street NE
Washington, DC 20002

For more information about our books, including a complete catalog, please write to us, call
1-800-374-2721, or visit our website at www.apa.org/pubs/magination.

Book design by Susan K. White
Printed by Worzalla, Stevens Point, WI

Library of Congress Cataloging-in-Publication Data

Glasser, Judith M.
Learning to feel good and stay cool : emotional regulation tools for kids with AD/HD /
by Judith M. Glasser, PhD and Kathleen Nadeau, PhD ; illustrated by Charles Beyl.
pages cm
Audience: 6-11.
ISBN 978-1-4338-1342-9 (hardcover) — ISBN 1-4338-1342-4 (hardcover) —
ISBN 978-1-4338-1343-6 (pbk.) — ISBN 1-4338-1343-2 (pbk.) 1. Attention-deficit-disordered
children—Juvenile literature. 2. Self-control in children—Juvenile literature. 3. Emotions in
children—Juvenile literature. I. Nadeau, Kathleen G. II. Beyl, Charles, illustrator. III. Title.
RJ506.H9G56 2014
618.92'8589—dc23   2013005779

Manufactured in the United States of America
10 9 8 7 6 5 4 3 2 1

Learning to Feel Good and Stay Cool

EMOTIONAL REGULATION TOOLS FOR KIDS WITH AD/HD

by Judith M. Glasser, PhD, and Kathleen Nadeau, PhD
illustrated by Charles Beyl

MAGINATION PRESS · WASHINGTON, DC
American Psychological Association

Contents

INTRODUCTION

TO PARENTS
AND OTHER ADULT HELPERS.................7
JUST FOR KIDS!.................9

CHAPTER 1
UNDERSTANDING YOUR FEELINGS.............11
Happy 14
Sad.................16
Interested.................16
Bored 17
Calm.................18
Angry.................19
Successful 20
Frustrated.................21
Proud 22
Ashamed 24
Determined.................24
Discouraged.................25
Connected.................26
Lonely.................27
Safe.................27
Scared.................28
Confident.................29
Worried.................30
Comfortable 30
Embarrassed.................31

CHAPTER 2
STAYING IN YOUR FEEL GOOD ZONE 33

Five Ways to Stay in Your Feel Good Zone........ 35
Feel Good Zone Habit #1: CH Is for CHill Out... 36
Feel Good Zone Habit #2: E Is for Exercise....... 38
Feel Good Zone Habit #3:
   E Is for Eat Healthy Protein 40
Feel Good Zone Habit #4: R Is for Routines...... 42
Feel Good Zone Habit #5: S Is for Sleep........... 46
Review 49

CHAPTER 3
STEERING CLEAR OF YOUR UPSET ZONE ..51

Knowing Your Warning Signs............................ 52
Dealing With Your Warning Signs..................... 54

CHAPTER 4
YOUR FEELINGS TOOLBOX 61

Feel Good Tools to Put in Your Feelings Toolbox...63
Feel Good Tools Review..................................... 71

CHAPTER 5
FEEL GOOD TOOLS
FOR SPECIFIC UPSET FEELINGS.................... 73

When You Feel Sad.. 74
When You Feel Bored 76
When You Feel Angry... 80
When You Feel Frustrated.................................. 83
When You Feel Ashamed 85

When You Feel Discouraged 89

When You Feel Lonely 91

When You Feel Scared 94

When You Feel Worried 96

When You Feel Embarrassed 98

My Action Plan 99

CHAPTER 6
PROBLEM-SOLVING
SO UPSETS COME LESS OFTEN 101

How to Be a Champion Problem-Solver 102

How Megan Solved Her Problem 104

CHAPTER 7
SPECIAL PROJECTS WITH MY PARENTS ... 109

Working Together on Changes 110

Step-by-Step Plan for Making Changes 114

Progress Chart 116

Reward Yourself! 118

NOTE TO PARENTS 119

Reward Your Child 120

Make a Clear Plan and Write It Down 121

Encourage Your Child 122

Plan Special Time With Your Child 123

Find the Resources That Your Child Needs 124

To Parents and Other Adult Helpers

LEARNING to manage emotions is one of the most important tasks of childhood. When your child cried as a baby, you could hold her, cuddle her, rock her, and sing to her to help calm her. Now that she is older, she needs to learn ways to soothe herself, especially when you aren't around to help. Children who learn to manage emotions tend to do better in school and to have an easier time getting along with others.

For kids with AD/HD, managing feelings can be even more challenging than it is for other kids. Kids with AD/HD tend to experience feelings more intensely than other kids do. When their feelings are *very* strong, it can be harder for them to control how they behave. Other people might feel that a child with AD/HD is "over-reacting" in a situation when he has such strong feelings. He may feel sad and retreat to his room, refusing to come out. If he feels very worried, he may beg to stay home from school, or even pretend to be sick. If he feels very angry, he may say and do things without thinking first. His feelings may rise to the surface instantly, leading to frequent conflicts and upset feelings.

Children with AD/HD often are less self-observant and more impulsive, making it harder for them to understand their feelings and develop emotional self-control. It is important for kids with AD/HD to develop an "early warning system" before feelings become too strong to control.

When a child is more aware of her feelings, she can take steps to calm down and feel better. This book offers practical tools, in terms that children can understand, to help them identify emotions, manage and reduce negative feelings, problem-solve so that upsets come less often, and develop daily habits that will help them feel good and function well.

Learning to Feel Good and Stay Cool is AD/HD-friendly. It is illustrated with cartoons to hold your child's interest, highly readable (even for kids who don't like to read), and divided into sections, so that the book can be read in smaller portions. It is intended for parents to read with their children. It can also be used as a guide by school counselors or other professionals who work with children.

This book introduces skills that can only become part of your child's daily life through active ongoing practice with you. Read this book with your child one chapter at a time. After each chapter, give your child time to integrate the ideas and put them into daily practice. Then, move on to the next chapter. Don't rush this process. Emphasize progress and do not dwell on failures. Work together to find ways to use the skills taught in this book more and more often.

Taking charge of our feelings instead of allowing them to take charge of us is a skill to learn early and practice throughout our lives. We hope this book is an enjoyable way for your child to begin learning and practicing this valuable life skill.

—Judith M. Glasser, PhD, and Kathleen Nadeau, PhD

Just for Kids!

EVERYBODY likes to feel good. When you feel good, everything usually goes better. For example, when you are happy, you probably smile at the people you meet and they probably smile back at you. Smiling makes you feel good and it makes the people around you feel good. When you feel happy, you get along better with other kids and with your family. Unfortunately, it isn't possible to feel good *all* the time. Everyone gets upset sometimes. It's normal to feel sad, angry, or frustrated when things in your life aren't going the way you want them to.

Many kids with AD/HD have really strong feelings that make it hard for them to control their behavior. Sometimes, their parents and other adults tell them that they are over-reacting. For example, a kid with AD/HD who feels very sad may run to his room, cry, and refuse to come out. His mother might think that the problem is really small, but to him, the problem feels really big.

A kid with AD/HD may feel so worried about school that she asks to stay home, or pretends to be sick. She might be worried that she will be in trouble for not finishing a project, or be afraid that she will fail a test.

When some kids with AD/HD feel very angry or hurt, it can be really hard for them to stop and think before they do or say things that get them in trouble with their family and friends.

Have any of these things ever happened to you? If so, you are not alone. Lots of other kids have trouble controlling their emotions too—even some adults! The good news is that there are skills you can learn to understand your emotions and feel better more often.

In this book we're going to teach you things you can do every day that will help you feel good. We'll also help you learn how to have fewer upsets, and we'll teach you lots of Feel Good Tools that you can use if you do feel upset or unhappy.

Have you ever seen a little child carry a blanket or a stuffed animal with him? He is starting to learn how to manage upset feelings. His stuffed toy or blanket is one of the first tools he has learned how to use to feel better when he is upset.

As kids get older, they don't usually carry around blankets or toys. They begin to learn other ways to calm down and feel better. Everyone feels upset or unhappy sometimes. You probably already know some good ways to feel better when you get upset. This book will teach you some more ways to feel good more often and strategies that will help you to stop feeling upset more quickly.

CHAPTER ONE

Understanding Your Feelings

EVERYBODY has feelings, starting from the time that they are tiny little babies. As babies grow up, they have to learn how to handle their feelings.

Everybody likes to feel good and everybody gets upset sometimes.

We wrote this book to help you understand what helps you have happy feelings and upset feelings. Sometimes, when you have AD/HD, your feelings are so strong that they are hard to handle. Even happy feelings can be hard to manage when they are very, very strong.

Just like some kids are good at reading but have trouble with math, some kids are good at managing their feelings, and some kids have more trouble. Some kids feel strong feelings more than others do—if you think of feelings being turned up like the volume dial on the radio, the "volume" is turned all the way up for kids with very strong feelings. Other kids have trouble controlling how they respond to their feelings. They may react without understanding why they feel the way they do.

The good news is that with practice, you can learn to manage your feelings better. This book will teach you some tools to understand what you are feeling and help you feel better when you start to get upset—like learning how to turn the volume down on your feelings dial.

Once you learn to do the things we'll teach you, you'll be able to feel good more of the time. And when you feel unhappy, you'll know what to do to feel better.

If you want to understand your feelings, first you need to know what to call them. When you were a little baby, you couldn't talk about your feelings. All you could do was cry when you felt tired or hungry or all alone. And when you felt good—like when your mom or dad fed you or hugged you or changed your diaper—you could smile and make little happy noises.

There are many different kinds of feelings. When you know what to call your feelings, you can begin to understand them. When you can talk about your feelings with other people, they can understand how you feel too. It can really feel good to talk about your feelings and have someone understand.

In the next few pages, we'll talk about feelings that lots of kids have. Let's see if you have some of these feelings, too.

Happy

Let's start with everyone's favorite feeling— happiness!

Some kids say that they get a warm feeling in their tummy when they are happy. Other kids say that they get a nice warm feeling all over. How do you feel inside when you feel happy?

Some kids feel happy when it's a snow day and they can stay home and play in the snow. Other kids feel happy when they are playing with friends, or when they get a big hug from their mom or dad.

Can you think of a time when you felt really happy? *Draw a picture of your happy memory here!*

Sad

Feeling sad is sort of the opposite of feeling happy.

Some kids say that when they feel sad their throat feels tight, as if they are about to cry. Or maybe they feel as if they want to lie down and curl up in a ball. How does your body feel when you feel sad?

Some kids feel sad when no one wants to play with them on the playground. Other kids feel sad because their mom or dad is far away from home.

Sometimes kids with AD/HD feel very sad because they make mistakes and their parents or teachers don't understand how hard they are trying.

Interested

Do you know what it's like to feel interested? When you are interested in something, you pay a lot of attention to it. Some kids say that when they are interested in something they feel wide awake. Their eyes are looking closely and their ears are listening closely. How do you feel inside when you are interested?

Kids sometimes feel very interested when they are listening to a really good story and want to know what happens next. Learning a new video game might make someone feel very interested. Or a kid might feel very interested when she sees a group of classmates talking and wonders what they are saying.

Kids with AD/HD can feel *very* interested in some things, and not at all interested in other things. Sometimes they are so interested in other things, they have trouble listening to the teacher or their parents.

Bored

Feeling bored is kind of the opposite of feeling interested.

Some kids say that when they are bored they feel like they're almost asleep. Other kids say that they feel like jumping out of their seat because they want to do something else. How do you feel inside when you are bored?

Sometimes school feels boring—like when the teacher is talking about something you are not interested in. Other kids say that they are bored when there is "nothing to do" or when it's a rainy day and they can't play outside.

Nobody likes to feel bored. In fact, many kids with AD/HD say that they hate to feel bored. Sometimes when they are bored they look for something more interesting instead of listening in school. Does this ever happen to you?

Calm

Calm is a pleasant, peaceful feeling. When everything is OK, we feel calm. When you feel calm your muscles are very relaxed. You might breathe more slowly and have a warm, peaceful feeling inside.

How do you feel inside when you are calm?

Some kids say that they feel calm when they are home sitting on the couch doing something that they enjoy. You might feel calm if you are sitting in the kitchen having a snack and talking to your mom or dad.

Some kids say that they feel cozy and calm when they are tucked in bed at night and their mom or dad is reading them a story.

Sometimes it's harder to feel calm when you have AD/HD because you have such strong upset feelings when little things go wrong every day.

Angry

Everyone feels angry sometimes.

Anger is an unpleasant feeling that can be hard to control, especially when you have AD/HD. Some kids say that they feel hot inside and their face gets red when they feel angry. Other kids say that they feel very tight and uncomfortable and feel like fighting or breaking things. How do you feel inside when you are angry?

What are some things that might make someone feel angry? Some kids feel angry when something doesn't seem fair. Other kids feel angry when someone yells at them or is mean to them.

Anger isn't a feeling that kids enjoy, but sometimes it can lead to something good. For example, you might feel angry when a friend doesn't treat you very well. Your anger might give you the strength to stand up to your friend or to look for a better friend instead of letting someone treat you badly.

Successful

Feeling successful is something that everyone likes. This is the feeling that you have inside when you have done something well. The harder you have to try to do something, the more successful you'll feel when you accomplish the task.

Some kids say that they feel successful when they learn to do something new, like ride a bike, write their name, or bake brownies. (Yum!) Kids feel especially successful when they have succeeded at something that was hard to do.

Some kids only want to do things they already know they can do. When kids have AD/HD, they often have trouble sticking with things that are hard for them until they succeed.

DAD NEVER LETS ME PICK THE MOVIES WE WATCH.

Frustrated

Feeling frustrated is unpleasant. You feel frustrated when things are not going your way or when you're having trouble doing something. When someone feels frustrated she might have a tight feeling in her head or neck. She might feel almost like crying, but it's not a sad feeling; she almost feels angry.

Sometimes kids say that they feel frustrated when they try and try to do something—like a hard math problem—but it keeps going wrong. Other kids feel frustrated when their mom or dad keeps telling them "no" when they want to do something.

If you have AD/HD, you might feel frustrated because lots of little things can go wrong when you have AD/HD. For example, you may feel frustrated if you forget to bring something to school that you need, or lose your homework after you've completed it. Other kids with AD/HD feel frustrated because they want to get their homework over with, but there is something they don't understand that is slowing them down.

Proud

Pride is a great feeling. When kids feel proud they feel good about themselves because of something that they have done well. What does it feel like inside when you feel proud? Some kids say that their chest feels bigger and they almost feel a little taller. It's a little like smiling inside.

Some kids say that they feel proud when they kick a goal when playing soccer, or when their team wins. Other kids feel proud when they learn to do something new, like ride a bike. Other kids feel proud when they try something new, even if they don't succeed at it right away.

Can you think of a time when you felt proud about something? *Draw a picture of yourself and your proud moment here.* You can look at this picture—and the picture of your happy memory—sometimes to remind yourself of your happy and proud feelings when things aren't going as well.

Ashamed

When you feel ashamed, you may feel as if you wish you could hide and no one could see you. It's the opposite of feeling proud. You may think that you have done something bad and that other people are saying negative things about you.

Some kids say that they feel ashamed because they feel badly about something that they have done—for example, if they have done something on purpose that is dishonest or hurtful.

Sometimes kids with AD/HD feel ashamed and blame themselves for mistakes even when they didn't do anything wrong.

Determined

Determination is a feeling that helps you keep trying, even when something is hard to do. What does it feel like inside when you are determined? Maybe you take strong deep breaths and tense your muscles so that you can work harder. Maybe your mind only thinks about trying hard, so that no discouraging thoughts can come in.

Some kids say that they feel more determined when someone is encouraging them to keep trying. Have you ever felt more determined because people clapped or cheered for your team? Some kids feel determined because they think encouraging thoughts that help them keep going.

Did you know that learning to feel determined can help you create moments when you feel proud and successful?

Discouraged

Feeling discouraged sometimes happens when you try hard, but still don't succeed. Everyone feels discouraged sometimes. Some kids say it's like they feel kind of tired and bad all over and want to quit trying. What does it feel like inside when you are discouraged?

Some kids say they feel discouraged if they go to a sports tryout and don't get chosen for the team. Or if they try and try to write a book report, but just can't think of what to say.

Sometimes, kids with AD/HD feel discouraged because teachers and parents don't think they're really trying. That can be really hard. In Chapter 5 we'll give you some ideas of things you can do when you feel discouraged.

Connected

Kids always feel better when they feel connected to other people. When we feel connected, we feel close to another person and know that they feel close to us, too.

Some kids say that they feel most connected when they are spending time with their best friend, or when they are hanging out at home with their family.

Many kids with AD/HD say that they feel more connected to people who understand them and what it's like to have AD/HD.

When you don't feel connected to other people, you can start feeling really lonely.

Lonely

Loneliness is a painful feeling, like feeling sad and all alone. When you feel lonely you may feel like there is a cloud over your head. When you feel lonely, you don't feel connected to others.

Some kids say that they feel lonely because they just moved to a new town and don't have any friends, or because they are home with a babysitter while their parents are at work all day. Sometimes you can even feel lonely when other people are around, if no one is noticing you or talking to you.

Safe

Safe is a wonderful feeling. Kids usually feel safe when they know that the grown-ups around them love them and will protect them and keep bad things from happening to them.

Sometimes kids say that they feel safe when they are with a parent or grandparent or even a big brother or sister—someone who they know will protect them and take care of them.

Scared

Feeling scared is the opposite of feeling safe. Children sometimes feel scared when they think that something bad might happen and they don't know what to do. When you feel scared you might have a bad feeling in your stomach. Your muscles might feel all tight like you want to run away. Some kids draw in their breath really fast or close their eyes when they feel really scared.

Some kids say that they feel scared when they are all alone in the house. You might feel scared if another kid says that he's going to hit you. Sometimes kids feel scared when they think that a grown-up will be mad at them about something.

There are lots of things you can learn to do to feel less scared. We'll teach you some of them in Chapter 5.

Confident

Everyone likes to feel confident. Confidence is sort of a calm, happy feeling we have when we are comfortable doing something and expect to do it well.

Some kids feel very confident when they give a report in front of the class because they are good at talking. Athletic kids feel confident when they play a sport. Some kids feel confident when they talk to other kids because they are good at making friends. Other kids feel confident that they will do well on a test at school because they studied hard to prepare for it.

Being successful at things helps us feel more confident when we try new things. It's important to do things that you are good at because it can help you feel more confident.

Worried

Feeling worried is kind of like being scared, but it is not as strong of a feeling. Kids can worry about lots of different things. Sometimes when kids worry their muscles feel tight. Worry can also give you a headache or cause your stomach to hurt. Worrying can make it hard to sleep or to pay attention in school.

Some kids worry that they won't do well in school, or that someone will become angry at them. Other kids worry about getting a shot at the doctor's office. Still other kids worry about monsters under their beds or in their closets at night.

In Chapter 5, we'll show you some ideas for how you can worry less.

Comfortable

When we feel comfortable, we feel relaxed and are not worried about anything.

Some kids feel comfortable when they are around people that they know and like. They may feel comfortable when they are home, just relaxing on the couch and hanging out with their family. Other kids say they feel comfortable when they are doing a quiet activity that they enjoy.

Embarrassed

Embarrassment is a feeling that nobody enjoys. It's a feeling that comes if you think that people are making fun of you.

When a kid feels embarrassed, his face may feel hot, and he may wish he could disappear so no one can look at him.

Kids feel embarrassed when they have done something that makes other kids laugh at them, like dropping a ball in a ball game, or making a mistake in front of the whole class.

Time for a Break!

Can you identify how our heroes are feeling based on their facial expressions?

__ confident   __ scared   __ angry   __ sad   __ embarrassed   __ happy

Wow! You've already learned a lot about feelings. It helps to know what to call your feelings so that you can talk about them and understand them better.

In this chapter, we have encouraged you to talk about times you had all sorts of feelings. That's because you'll start feeling better when you talk to someone about unhappy feelings. And it feels great to share good feelings, too!

The more you share your feelings, the more connected you'll feel to other people. And feeling connected is a great feeling to have.

Good for you! You've made a great start!

CHAPTER TWO

Staying in Your Feel Good Zone

HAVE you ever thought about why something upsets you at one time, but when the same thing happens at a different time you feel pretty calm?

For example, think of the times when your little brother or sister played with something that belongs to you. Sometimes, you might react calmly and remind them that they need to ask first. Other times, you might grab your toy, yell, and feel very angry.

When you're in your "Feel Good Zone," things bother you less. But when you're in your "Upset Zone," even little things can cause big upsets.

In this chapter, we're going to teach you about how to stay in your Feel Good Zone more of the time.

Five Ways to Stay in Your Feel Good Zone

 Chill Out! Chill out and relax at least once a day.

 Exercise. Get active exercise every day.

 Eat Healthy Protein so your brain has the fuel it needs.

 Routines. Create daily routines so you feel more calm and organized.

Sleep. Get at least 9–10 hours of sleep each night.

A good way to remember how to stay in your Feel Good Zone is to remember the word **CHEERS!**

Get it?

CHill Out

Exercise

Eat Healthy Protein

Routines

Sleep

Three **CHEERS** for staying in your Feel Good Zone!

FEEL GOOD ZONE HABIT #1:

CH Is for Chill Out!

You'll stay in your Feel Good Zone more of the time when you are feeling calm, cool, and relaxed. Here are some ways to chill out and stay cool every day.

Have "down time" every day. Down time is time to relax. Some kids have so many activities that they don't have any down time. If you don't have much down time, talk to your parents and ask them if you can cut back on some of your activities. If you want to stay in your Feel Good Zone, be sure that you have some down time to relax every day.

Meditate a few minutes every day. Meditation is a special way to calm down and chill out. Pick a special place and a special time of day to learn to meditate. Practice with your mom or dad.

To meditate, sit quietly and pay attention to your breathing. You can focus your mind on the rise and fall of your chest as you breathe, or on the air as it goes in of your nose or mouth. You can close your eyes or put an object in front of you to look at. Whenever your thoughts wander, bring them back and focus on your breathing once again or on the object in front of you. Try this for 10 minutes each day. See Feel Good Tool #9 on page 69 for more instructions.

One way to learn how to meditate is to follow along with a meditation CD. (See the list of meditation CDs for kids at the back of this book.)

Take a "green break" every day. Take a few minutes and go outside and spend time in nature—in your yard, at a park, or on a walk. Try to play outside every day.

Remember these three ways to chill out!
- Down time
- Meditation
- Green breaks

Pick your favorite, or try all three!

FEEL GOOD ZONE HABIT #2:

E Is for Exercise!

It's important to exercise every day to produce more of the brain chemicals that help you to feel good, think clearly, and problem-solve. The best exercise for your brain is aerobic exercise—any exercise that keeps your heart beating fast. Walking fast, running, and riding your bike are all good ways to get aerobic exercise. After a half-hour of aerobic exercise, wonderful things start happening in your brain that help you to feel better, focus better, and learn better!

Make exercise a part of your regular routine.
Talk to your mom or dad about ways that you can get more exercise, like:

- going for a bike ride
- doing after-school sports
- running around with your friends outside

Find exercises you can do indoors. Exercise is *so* important that you should find ways to do it every day, even when there is bad weather outside. Talk to your mom or dad about ways you can exercise indoors, like:

- running up and down the stairs 15 times
- using a treadmill (if your family has one)
- jumping for 15 minutes on an indoor trampoline (if your family has one)
- watching an exercise DVD for kids and following along
- playing an exercise Wii game (if your family has one)
- running in place for 15 minutes while you watch TV
- dancing to music

Make exercise more fun. If you enjoy exercising, you will be more likely to do it every day! Here are some ways to make exercising more enjoyable:

- Listen to fast music while you exercise—music can really get you going!
- Follow along with a kids' exercise DVD.
- Exercise with a friend or family member— it is important for grown-ups, too!
- Reward yourself for exercising each day. Talk to your mom or dad about what reward you'd like.

Whatever activity you choose to do, it will help you feel good. Moving your body helps you feel calm and happy and is really good for your brain!

FEEL GOOD ZONE HABIT #3:

E Is for Eat Healthy Protein!

Fuel for your brain comes from the food you eat. Eating things that are sweet or starchy (such as bread, sweet cereal, chips, and candy) give your brain too much fuel that runs out quickly. And when your brain fuel runs out, you are more likely to get upset and feel cranky.

To keep your brain's fuel tank full all day long, you need to eat protein at every meal. Protein comes from:

- eggs
- milk
- cheese
- peanut butter
- nuts
- tuna fish (and other kinds of fish)
- chicken
- hamburgers
- rice and beans
- protein drinks
- protein bars

Eat healthy food with protein all day long. Ask an adult before trying any new food, to make sure that it is safe to eat and good for you. Here are some ideas for how to eat healthy protein throughout the day:

- **Breakfast**
  Your brain needs a jump start in the morning with a breakfast of protein and carbohydrates, like eggs and toast or non-sugary cereal and milk.
- **At school**
  Be sure to pack a lunch and snacks that have protein in them, such as a PB & J or a chicken sandwich. This will keep your brain going all day long.
- **After school**
  When you get home from school have a good snack of something like nut butter and fruit to keep you going until dinner.

- **Dinner**
  More protein at dinner will keep you going while you do your homework.
- **Bedtime snack**
  A bedtime snack of milk and crackers can help you feel calm and fall asleep more quickly.
- **Water, water, water!**
  And don't forget water! We think more clearly when we drink plenty of water.

Food is fuel for your brain, so feed your brain well!

FEEL GOOD ZONE HABIT #4:

R Is for Routines!

Routines are important for staying in your Feel Good Zone. If you don't have a routine to follow, you are more likely to get stressed out and frustrated. Then pretty soon you'll be heading into your Upset Zone.

If you follow your routine, you won't have to rush and feel stressed. Following routines will help you know where your things are when you need them. Following routines will make it easier to eat in a healthy way and get plenty of sleep so that you will feel better.

It is important to build morning, after-school, and bedtime routines into your daily life. The following routines are examples. Talk to your mom or dad about developing the routine that works best for you. Make charts with your mom or dad to remind you of your daily routines. Hang the chart where you will always see it.

Sample Feel Good Morning Routine

1. Get up at least one hour before you need to leave the house.

2. Get up about the same time every morning, even on weekends.

3. Get dressed.

4. Eat a healthy breakfast that includes protein.

5. Brush your teeth.

6. Gather everything you need for the day.

7. Don't get sidetracked by watching TV or playing with something until you are *completely* ready to head out the door.

8. Plan to leave ten minutes early so you are not in a rush.

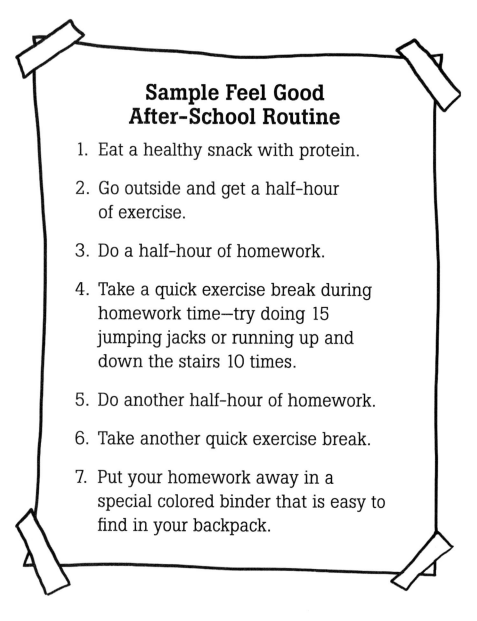

Sample Feel Good
After–School Routine

1. Eat a healthy snack with protein.

2. Go outside and get a half–hour of exercise.

3. Do a half–hour of homework.

4. Take a quick exercise break during homework time—try doing 15 jumping jacks or running up and down the stairs 10 times.

5. Do another half–hour of homework.

6. Take another quick exercise break.

7. Put your homework away in a special colored binder that is easy to find in your backpack.

On days that you have after-school activities, get a snack and start on homework as soon as you get home.

Finish your homework each day, then reward yourself with a favorite activity.

Sample Feel Good
Bedtime Routine

1. Start your bedtime routine one hour before bedtime.

2. Lay out your clothes for the next day.

3. Gather everything you will need for the next day and put it with your backpack in a special place where you will see it as you get ready to leave in the morning.

4. Eat a bedtime snack of milk and crackers.

5. Brush your teeth.

6. Take a warm bath or shower.

7. Put on your pajamas.

8. Get into bed and read or ask your mom or dad to read to you.

9. Turn out the light at the same time each night.

10. Listen to soft music while you go to sleep.

FEEL GOOD ZONE HABIT #5:

S Is for Sleep!

If you want to stay in your Feel Good Zone, you need to get plenty of sleep. Lots of kids tell us that they have a very hard time falling asleep at night. They turn out the light and just lie there, unable to go to sleep.

If this describes you, here are some things you can do to fall asleep.

Do a calm-down exercise before bed. Did you know that cats sleep about 16 hours a day? They know a lot about sleep!

Imagine yourself as a cat sleeping in a warm spot in your house, maybe where the sun comes streaming in the window.

Curl up in your warm blanket and make a nest, then feel the warmth of the sun all over your body. Before you know it you may feel warm all over and very sleepy.

You could also close your eyes and imagine that you are on Sleepy Hill.

Sleepy Hill is a beautiful place on a hillside. It is always sunny there, and just the right temperature for you—not too cold and not too hot. There is a big, shady tree on the top of Sleepy Hill and a big, thick, comfortable blanket for you to lie down on. Lying down on the blanket under the tree, you look up at the blue sky in front of you with big, puffy white clouds floating above you. A warm, gentle breeze brings with it wonderful smells, like fresh cut grass or your favorite flowers. Maybe you see interesting shapes in those clouds above you. You imagine what it would be like to be floating on your favorite cloud in the sky. As you relax, you know that there are people on Sleepy Hill who are watching over you and making sure that you are completely safe and comfortable. No one can disturb you on Sleepy Hill. You can let yourself completely relax and drift off into a restful sleep.

Get exercise every day. Daily exercise will help you go to sleep at night.

Avoid caffeine in the afternoon or evening. Drinks with caffeine include some soft drinks, tea, coffee, and even hot chocolate. Caffeine wakes your brain up so that it's hard to fall asleep.

Don't have "screen time" for one hour before bed. "Screen time" means any time you spend in front of the TV, computer, cell phone, or other screens. Did you know that sitting in front of a TV or computer screen stops your brain from getting sleepy?

Go through your bedtime routine at the same time every night. This helps your body get used to the same sleep schedule. Try going to bed at the same time each night, and getting up at the same time each morning, even on the weekends.

Sweet dreams!

Review

Pick one Feel Good Zone Habit at a time and work on it with your mom or dad. When the habit you have chosen is going pretty well, then pick another habit to help you stay in your Feel Good Zone.

 CHill Out

 Exercise

 Eat Healthy Protein

 Routines

 Sleep

CHEERS!

Which one Feel Good Zone Habit would you like to start with? Pick one and get started today. Pretty soon you'll be in your Feel Good Zone Habit most of the time!

Time for a Break!

Can you find the words that are hidden in the word search below?

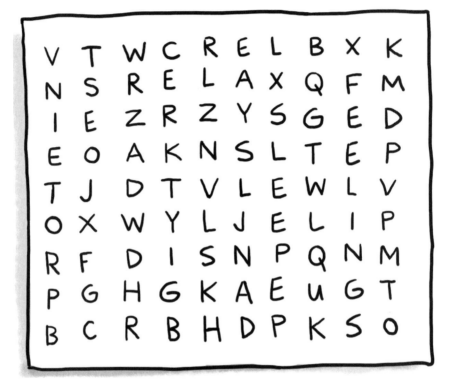

```
V  T  W  C  R  E  L  B  X  K
N  S  R  E  L  A  X  Q  F  M
I  E  Z  R  Z  Y  S  G  E  D
E  O  A  K  N  S  L  T  E  P
T  J  D  T  V  L  E  W  L  V
O  X  W  Y  L  J  E  L  I  P
R  F  D  I  S  N  P  Q  N  M
P  G  H  G  K  A  E  U  G  T
B  C  R  B  H  D  P  K  S  O
```

RELAX   SLEEP

CHILL   EAT

FEELINGS   PROTEIN

CHAPTER THREE

Steering Clear of Your Upset Zone

IN Chapter 2, we discussed how sometimes you feel very upset when your brother or sister plays with your toys, but at other times the same thing happens and you only feel a little upset.

You are more likely to get upset if you are already heading toward your Upset Zone. When people are in their Upset Zone, even little things can feel like big problems.

You can't always stay out of your Upset Zone, but there are warning signs that can tell you that you're getting close. In this chapter, we're going to teach you about those warning signs so that you can pay attention to them and avoid your Upset Zone more often.

When you pay attention to your warning signs, you'll be able to avoid lots of big upsets and stay in your Feel Good Zone more of the time.

Knowing Your Warning Signs

Your warning signs are situations that make it more likely you will be pushed into your Upset Zone. Here are some things that send kids toward their Upset Zone. Check off the ones that apply to you.

I am more likely to head toward my Upset Zone when:

- ☐ I feel really hungry.
- ☐ I feel tired.
- ☐ I had a hard day at school.
- ☐ I feel rushed.
- ☐ I feel frustrated about my homework.
- ☐ I feel antsy because I've been indoors all day long.
- ☐ I feel sick.
- ☐ Someone keeps bugging me.
- ☐ I am worried about something.
- ☐ I have upset feelings that I keep inside.
- ☐ I don't have any time to relax.

Can you think of other situations that push you closer to your Upset Zone? Talk to your mom or dad or another adult about them. It can help if you make a list of your warning signs. On the next page, you can write down any warning signs from the list above that apply to you, or any other situations that make you feel more upset. That way you'll be more likely to notice them when they happen.

The more you understand the warning signs that tell you you're getting closer to your Upset Zone, the better you will become at avoiding upsets.

MY WARNING SIGNS:

Dealing With Your Warning Signs

Once you notice a warning sign, it's important to do something so that you don't get pushed into your Upset Zone. Here are examples of what you could do when you notice a warning sign from the list above.

When I feel hungry, I'll get something healthy to eat right away.

When I feel tired, I will lie down and rest a while.

If that isn't possible (for example, if I'm at school), I will do stretches to wake myself up. I will try to rest as soon as possible, or make a plan to go to bed early that night.

When I've had a hard day at school, I will talk about it with Mom or Dad.

When I feel rushed in the morning, I will slow down for a minute, close my eyes, think "calm down and stay cool," and then promise myself I'll follow my morning routine tomorrow.

When I feel frustrated with my homework, I'll take a break and then ask for some help.

When I feel antsy because I've been inside all day, I'll go outside or do some indoor exercises.

When I feel sick, I'll tell Mom or Dad so that they can help me. Then I'll lie down in a quiet place.

When my brother or sister keeps bugging me, I'll ignore them and go somewhere else for a while.

When I'm worried about something, I'll talk to Mom or Dad or another grown-up about it so that they can help me problem-solve.

When I'm holding upset feelings inside, I'll write them down in a journal or talk to Mom or Dad about them.

When I feel like I never have time to relax, I'll talk to my mom or dad about my schedule. Maybe I need to have fewer after-school activities.

These are just some ideas about warning signs and what to do about them. Can you think of others? Look back at your list of warning signs on page 54, and try to think of something you can do about each one.

WAYS TO DEAL WITH MY
WARNING SIGNS:

Let's read about Jake and how he learned to pay attention to his warning signs and stay away from his Upset Zone.

Jake had a hard day at school. He didn't do very well on his math quiz. After school, his coach yelled at the whole team about not working hard enough. And when he got home he was starving, but dinner wasn't ready yet.

Jake knew that he needed to be careful so he wouldn't go into his Upset Zone. He had three warning signs about situations that might send him into his Upset Zone:

- He was hungry.
- He was upset because the coach had yelled.
- He was worried about his math grade.

Here's what Jake did to stay out of his Upset Zone.

- First, as soon as he got home, Jake grabbed an apple and a cheese stick and went to chill out in his room.
- After he felt better, he talked to his mother about his math quiz. She offered to help with math after dinner.
- At dinner, he told his parents that the coach had yelled at the team. Jake felt better after his parents told him they were proud of how hard he was trying.

Jake felt much calmer and was able to settle down and work on his math homework after dinner.

Before Jake learned about his warning signs, he might have had a big argument with someone when he came home. Now, Jake knows his warning signs and what to do about them. Instead of having an upset after his hard day, Jake calmed down, enjoyed having dinner with his family, and was able to do his math homework with help from his mom.

Just like Jake, you can understand the warning signs that you are getting close to your Upset Zone. Next time you start feeling a little upset, see if you can recognize some warning signs. Remember what Jake did. Try to identify your warning signs and figure out what to do about them.

The more you learn about your warning signs, the less time you'll spend in your Upset Zone!

Time for a Break!

Can you find your way from the Upset Zone to the Feel Good Zone?

CHAPTER FOUR

Your Feelings Toolbox

EVERYONE has Feel Good Tools. Feel Good Tools are ways that we help ourselves to stay in our Feel Good Zone. Feel Good Tools can also help you to feel better when you are upset.

Have you ever noticed when little kids feel upset that they sometimes suck their thumbs or hold onto a favorite stuffed animal? Their thumbs and their stuffed animals are their first Feel Good Tools. They are just beginning to learn how to calm down and feel better.

Little kids don't have many tools in their Feelings Toolbox, but you are older and you have probably learned some other ways to help yourself feel better when you feel sad or upset or angry.

What are some of the Feel Good Tools that you use to help yourself feel better? Maybe if you sit down with your mom or dad or another grown-up they can help you think of some of your Feel Good Tools.

In addition, we're going to teach you more Feel Good Tools.

Pick the tools you like best and practice them until you are really good at them. Later, you can come back and pick other Feel Good Tools to practice.

The more tools you have in your Feelings Toolbox, the easier it will be to feel good and stay calm.

Feel Good Tools to Put in Your Feelings Toolbox

In this section, we'll talk about Feel Good Tools that can help you feel better in all kinds of situations. Use these tools every day and you'll stay in your Feel Good Zone more of the time.

Feel Good Tool #1:

Talk to someone about how you feel. No matter what the problem is, you'll always feel better if you tell someone how you feel. When you talk to someone, you won't feel all alone with your unhappy feelings. Being close to other people and telling them your feelings will help you feel better fast.

Feel Good Tool #2:

Laugh a lot. Laughter will always help you feel better. The fastest way to go from unhappy to happy is to laugh out loud. Remember, though, that it may not always be appropriate to laugh out loud (for example, in the middle of class). Think about the things that can make you feel like laughing. Here are some ideas:

- Watch a funny show on TV.
- Have a silly pillow fight with your brother or sister.
- Ask your mom or dad to chase and tickle you.

When you are laughing it is hard to feel scared or upset at the same time.

Feel Good Tool #3:
Take a green break. A "green break" is time that you spend outside just chilling out or doing something that you like. We call it a green break because it's important to spend time around green nature—grass and bushes and trees.

Whether you just sit in the yard, go to a park, or go for a short walk, you'll feel better after a few minutes.

So next time you're feeling a little stressed out, instead of staying inside, if the weather is nice, get outside and let nature help you feel better. Always let an adult know if you want to leave the house.

Feel Good Tool #4:
Listen to music. Music can help you feel better fast. Slow, calm music can help you feel calmer. And music with a happy tune can cheer you up. What's your favorite kind of music?

Dancing to music is even better! It's almost impossible to feel upset while you're dancing to happy music.

So remember, next time you want to calm down or cheer up, turn on the music!

Feel Good Tool #5:
Draw or paint about your feelings. When you don't know how to describe your feelings with words, it really helps to draw or paint your feelings.

Once you get your unhappy feelings out of your head and onto the paper, you'll feel much better.

The movements you make while you draw or paint can help you calm down too.

Feel Good Tool #6:

Get some exercise to feel better fast. Exercise is a great way to feel better fast. If you are frustrated with your homework, try standing up and doing 10 or 15 jumping jacks—just enough so that you are panting a little bit. Then sit down and try your homework again.

We bet you'll feel calmer and more relaxed. Every time you feel yourself getting frustrated or tired of sitting in your chair, get up and do some more jumping jacks.

Walking or riding your bike for a few minutes will also help you feel better. So remember, don't just sit there and feel unhappy—get moving!

Feel Good Tool #7:
Go to your "cooling off" space. A "cooling off" space is any place in your house where you can go away from everyone and be calm and quiet for a few minutes.

Think about where you would like your cooling off space to be at home. It could be in your bedroom, or even a cozy space with pillows behind a couch or chair.

Wherever you choose for your cooling off space, it should be quiet and comfy. Then, whenever you feel upset or unhappy, try going to your cooling off space. If you want to, try doing a quiet activity like reading a book or playing with a toy.

We bet you'll soon feel much better.

Feel Good Tool #8:
Do something that you enjoy. Doing an activity that you enjoy is a great way to get your mind off of your upset feelings. Sometimes we stay upset because we keep thinking about the thing that made us unhappy. Doing something that you enjoy, whether it is an inside activity, like building with Legos, or something outdoors, like shooting hoops, will give your brain something new to think about.

If you move your thoughts away from your unhappy feelings for a little while, you'll start to feel better.

What are some activities that could help you feel better?

MY FAVORITE ACTIVITIES:

Feel Good Tool #9:

Meditate. If you meditate for a few minutes every day, you'll feel good because you have trained your brain to be calm.

In some schools they even teach kids to meditate in class because it can help kids to calm down and pay better attention. Ready to try it?

Sit on the floor in a quiet place with your legs crossed and your hands on your knees.

Now, close your eyes and sit quietly. Just think about breathing in and out. If you start thinking about something else, just think about your breathing again.

Lots of kids can meditate more easily when they listen to a special recording that plays soft music along with a person's voice that slowly reminds you what to do while you meditate.

Here are some more ways you can meditate:

Walking meditation. We know that some kids with AD/HD might have trouble sitting still to meditate. If you try it and it doesn't work for you, it might help if you do a walking meditation: go for a slow walk and concentrate on what it feels like to take each step and to breathe in and out. You might notice what it feels like outside, if there is a warm sun and a nice breeze.

Eating meditation. Peel an orange. Focus on the smell and feel of the orange peel. Put the orange segment in your mouth all at once. Close your eyes. Bite down and feel the juice burst into your mouth. Notice how it feels and how it tastes.

Painting or coloring meditation. In this kind of meditation, you color in a coloring book while saying something over and over in your mind, like "I am calm and I am in control." Coloring while you repeat this phrase can help you to stay cool and calm.

Maybe your mom or dad can get you a special coloring book like *Power Mandalas* (see page 126). This book has drawings to color in and things to say to help you meditate while you draw.

There are some books and CDs listed in the back of this book if you and your parents would like to learn more about meditation.

Feel Good Tool # 10:

Check your "warning signs." Remember when we talked about your warning signs that you are moving toward your Upset Zone? The closer you come to your Upset Zone, the easier it is for a little problem to cause a big upset.

So, if you are starting to feel just a little upset, check your warning signs. If you're hungry, eat a snack. If you're feeling tired, lie down or even take a little nap. The more you learn to pay attention to your warning signs, the less often you'll have big upsets when a problem comes along.

Feel Good Tools Review

We've talked about a lot of different Feel Good Tools that can help you feel better whenever you feel unhappy. Let's make a list so that you can remember them.

- Talk to someone about how you feel.
- Laugh a lot.
- Take a green break.
- Listen to music.
- Draw or paint about your feelings.
- Get some exercise to feel better fast.
- Go to your "cooling off space."
- Do something that you enjoy.
- Meditate.
- Check your "warning signs."

Wow! That's a lot of tools that you can use to feel good.

If you like, you can write down this list and keep it where you can see it so you'll know what to do when you want to feel better.

Time for a Break!

Taking a green break is an important Feel Good Tool. See if you can spot the differences between these two scenes.

CHAPTER FIVE

Feel Good Tools for Specific Upset Feelings

IN this chapter, we're going to teach you about Feel Good Tools that work with specific kinds of upset feelings. Not all unhappy feelings are the same. Some Feel Good Tools work best with certain kinds of upset feelings.

After you read this section, you'll know more about what to do to feel better fast when something is upsetting you.

When You Feel SAD

Can you think of some times when you felt sad? It's natural to feel sad sometimes. Here are some things you can do to feel better when you feel sad.

Ask for a hug. Everyone feels better after a hug!

Talk to someone about why you feel sad. You'll feel better if you share your feelings with someone.

Smile. Smiling, even when you feel sad, can help you feel better. When you smile at other people, they smile back and you both feel better!

Pull a happy memory from your happy memory bag. Start a collection of happy memories right now, so that you can pull them out when you need them!

Write down your list of happy memories. Maybe your mom or dad can help you remember them and write them down.

Do a "happy activity" to put yourself in a better mood. Here are some activities that other kids have suggested for getting into a good mood:

- Watch a funny TV show.
- Have a silly pillow fight with your brother or sister.
- Watch your favorite happy movie.
- Ask for a tickle from your mom or dad.
- Talk to a friend on the phone.
- Play some happy music and dance around.

We bet that you can think of some more happy activities. Keep a list where you can see it next time you feel sad.

When You Feel BORED

Nobody likes to feel bored, but for some kids with AD/HD being bored is especially hard. Here are a few ideas for how to feel bored less of the time:

When you are at school:

Participate. If you feel bored at school, try participating instead of just sitting back and feeling bored. We usually feel more interested in things when we actively participate. Try raising your hand to answer the teacher's question, or raise your hand to respond to what another student has said. Or ask a question. Get involved!

Write down what you hear. Another way to participate and feel less bored is to write down what your teacher is saying. You have to pay close attention so that you know what to write down— and paying close attention will keep you from feeling bored.

Earn interesting activities by completing your work. If you feel bored at school because you finish your work sooner than other students, talk to your parents and your teacher. Make an agreement that if you finish your work and do a good job on it that you can go do something you like somewhere in the classroom until the other students finish, if your teacher allows it.

Use fidget objects. Keep quiet fidget objects at your desk, like a springy pencil topper or a stress ball. (Your parents can get some fidget objects for you.) Sometimes it's easier to sit quietly when you're bored if you have something to do with your hands.

When you are stuck in a boring situation:

Sometimes you have to sit through an event, such as a play, concert, or wedding, that you may not find interesting. Here are a few ideas for when you're stuck in a boring situation.

Try listening. See if you can understand what is being talked about. Actually trying to listen instead of just waiting for the situation to be over will help you feel less bored.

Do a quiet activity. Ask your parents if you can do a quiet activity that won't bother anyone else. You'll need to plan ahead to have something to do. Sometimes just having a pencil and a piece of paper can help a lot because you can doodle and draw.

Use fidget objects. Bring a quiet fidget object along—like a stress ball to squeeze while you sit and wait. Of course you have to be careful that your fidgeting doesn't bother others!

Invent a quiet game. For example, see how long you can go without moving. Time yourself, then see if you can beat your record.

Daydream! This is a perfect situation for daydreaming—what would be fun to think about? Something fun you love to do? Your favorite vacation?

When you feel bored at home because it feels like there is nothing to do or no one to play with:

There is always something to do! The trick is to learn how to think of interesting things to do. Some kids get so used to being entertained by the television or their computer that they aren't in the habit of thinking of other things to do.

Make a list. Sometime when you aren't bored, make a list of interesting things to do when there is no TV, no computer to play on, or no one to play with. Post the list in your room to remind yourself next time you are bored.

Be creative. Being "creative" means making something up by yourself. You could create a story, a poem, a drawing, or a structure made of Legos or building blocks.

Practice imagining. Imagining means "seeing" things in your thoughts. For example, you could imagine a school where you had recess five times a day! Or a school with water slides! Let your imagination think of amazing things. You definitely won't be bored!

Play by yourself. Collect some toys or games that you enjoy playing alone so that you have something to do when there is no one else to play with.

When You Feel ANGRY

Anger is a very upsetting feeling. Kids may feel anger when they think that somebody has been mean or unfair to them. Do you ever feel this way? Sometimes kids with AD/HD feel such strong angry feelings that it's hard not to lose control.

Here are some ways to calm down your anger when you feel as if you're about to explode.

Calm down your volcano. Do you ever feel so angry that you feel as if you are about to explode like a volcano? Here is a way to start feeling calmer fast.

Look for a quiet place to go. A good idea is to think of a "cooling off space" where you can go when you get upset. This is a place where you keep a basket of things that help you calm down, like a pillow or stuffed animal, a coloring book, or a puzzle book. Breathe very slowly, in and out, ten times. Say "calm" when you breathe in and "relax" when you breathe out, quietly to yourself. Stay there until you feel calm.

Imagine that your anger is a big volcano with smoke coming out the top. Suppose that the smoke gradually stops. Keep breathing in and out very slowly. Now, imagine that the volcano is becoming a beautiful peaceful mountain with green grass and a blue sky above it. As your anger volcano turns into a pretty green mountain, keep breathing in and out until you feel calm.

"Un-stick" yourself from an argument. Some kids get stuck in arguments and can't seem to stop. Do you get "stuck" in an argument sometimes? When people keep arguing, they become more and more angry.

When you have AD/HD, it can be harder to walk away from an argument. Tell yourself. "Stop, stop, stop! This is just my AD/HD bothering me!" Then go away and do something else for a while. You are more likely to solve the problem if you talk when you feel calmer.

Be smart and leave before a fight can start! Little problems can turn into big problems when kids feel angry. Angry words can quickly turn into a fight. If you feel very angry because someone has said or done something mean, go away quickly. Stay away from the person that is trying to start a fight. If that person won't leave you alone after you try to go away, tell a grown-up. Tell yourself you are not going to let another kid get you in trouble.

Stay away from kids who are mean to you or tease you! Some kids make fun of other kids. They tease them or call them names. If you know someone who is doing this to you, try to stay away from him or her.

Put yourself in the other person's shoes.
Sometimes, when you feel angry about something, you only think about your own upset. If you think about why the other person is upset, sometimes

you'll understand why they behaved the way they did. Then you might not feel so angry any more. We call this "putting yourself in their shoes."

When You Feel FRUSTRATED

Kids with AD/HD often feel frustrated, so it's really important to learn to manage your frustrated feelings. You feel frustrated when something is stopping you from getting to something you want or when little things keep going wrong. Let's look at what you can do about your frustrated feelings.

Problem-solve. Sometimes you can use your problem-solving skills to make your situation better. Figure out what is causing you frustration and try to brainstorm some solutions. For example, if you are feeling frustrated because you lost your homework, talk to your mom or dad about ways to get organized for school at night, so you have what you need when you leave in the morning. If you feel frustrated because you can't watch TV until you finish your homework, ask your mom and dad if you can record the show you're missing. If you keep making mistakes on your homework, ask for help.

Slow down. It's a funny thing, but often when we try to rush through a task it ends up taking longer. You may want to get your homework or chores over with quickly, but if you rush through them you may make mistakes and have to start over. A good thing to tell yourself when you are rushing is, "Slow is fast and fast is slow." That means that when you slow down and pay attention to your task, you'll end up doing it right the first time and be done with it sooner.

Shift your attention. Kids with AD/HD often have trouble waiting. That's because they keep thinking about the thing that they are waiting for, so the time seems to move more slowly. Instead, figure out a way to think about something else and you'll be surprised at how quickly the time passes. When you're going somewhere like a doctor's appointment where you know you'll probably have to wait, always take something with you to do, like a book or magazine to read. If you're paying attention to your book or magazine, you won't be thinking about the wait and won't feel as frustrated.

Similarly, you may also feel frustrated when you want something and your mom or dad tells you "no." If you keep thinking about the thing you want and keep asking for it over and over, you'll just keep your frustrated feelings going. This is when it is a good idea to say, "STOP" to yourself, to remind yourself that this is just your AD/HD taking charge of your brain. Picture a big, red stop sign. Then think about one of your happiest memories or something you are really looking forward to doing.

This may sound hard to do, but it is really important to learn to shift your attention to another thing instead of staying stuck in frustration.

For example, Carlos was trying to do his homework. He was getting really frustrated because he didn't understand what to do. When the teacher was giving the instructions, he was thinking about his baseball game the day before. Carlos realized he was getting into his Upset Zone and he remembered what to do. First he went outside to take a short bike ride. While he was doing that, he thought, "I can call Sam. He might know what we are supposed to do." So he went home and called Sam. Sam explained the homework and Carlos finished it. Then he went out to play with his friends.

Way to go, Carlos!

When You Feel ASHAMED

Shame is a feeling that nobody likes to feel. When you feel ashamed because you are concerned that you have done something that hurts someone else, here are some things you can do to start feeling better:

Ask yourself if you've done something wrong.
If you are not sure, talk to a grown-up that you trust and see what she thinks.

Try to make up for it. For example, if you have taken something without permission, give it back. If you have broken something, pay for it or replace it.

Apologize. If you have done something that has hurt someone else, say you're sorry. Talk to a grown-up about what to say when you apologize.

For example, James took some candy at the store when no one was looking and put it in his pocket. Once he got home, he felt really ashamed of himself. He couldn't even enjoy the candy. So James thought about it and decided to tell his mom. His mom took him right back to the store and he told the manager what he had done and returned the candy. He felt embarrassed while he was talking to the manager, but after he returned home he felt much better. His mom even told him she was proud of him for being honest about what he had done.

Sometimes, we feel ashamed because we have done something that makes us feel badly about ourselves, even though it doesn't harm anyone else. Here are some things you can do to feel better:

Imagine your best friend did the same thing. Ask yourself, "Would I blame my best friend for the same thing?" If you wouldn't blame your best friend, then it's important to be just as kind and understanding toward yourself.

Remind yourself that nobody is perfect. Tell yourself that you don't need to feel ashamed because you're not perfect.

Think about ways you could change your behavior. If you feel ashamed about something that you would like to change about yourself, think about behavior that you can change.

For example, Susan felt ashamed because she kept losing things. This problem was also causing her to feel frustrated a lot of the time. She talked to her school counselor about her problem, and she learned that she was not alone. Her school counselor told her that lots of kids have this problem. Susan also talked to her mom about this problem and her mom reminded her that no one is perfect, and that everyone has areas in which they could improve.

After she talked to her school counselor and her mom, Susan felt less ashamed. Then she talked to them about how to solve the problem. Her mom helped her get her room organized so she would have a place for all her important things. Then Susan decided to remind herself that if she took the time to put her things back in their special places, she would save time later looking for them!

Her school counselor helped Susan find a friend who she could check in with every day to make sure she had everything she needed to do her homework each night.

With her mom and dad's help, Susan figured out ways to reward herself for keeping track of her stuff. When she did she felt very proud of herself!

When You Feel DISCOURAGED

Do you ever feel discouraged? Everyone feels discouraged sometimes. If you feel discouraged a lot of the time, it's time to learn some Feel Good Tools that can help your discouragement go away.

Here are some ways to feel better when you feel discouraged.

Encourage yourself. Do you know the story of "The Little Engine That Could"? This story is a great example of how to encourage yourself.

The Little Blue Engine was trying to carry a big load up a steep mountain. All the way up the mountain, the Little Blue Engine was huffing and puffing. It was very hard, but she encouraged herself saying, "I think I can! I think I can!" until finally she reached the top.

You can learn to encourage yourself, too. Just like the little engine, if you tell yourself you can do it, you'll keep trying.

Replace negative thoughts with positive ones.
Do you ever have negative thoughts like "I'm dumb,"
or "It's all my fault"?

Next time, try changing your negative thoughts to
positive ones. Here are some ideas:

- "I'm not dumb! I'll figure it out!"
- "No big deal! I'll ask for help."
- "I can do it if I try!"
- "Everybody makes mistakes sometimes."

As soon as your thoughts are positive, your feelings
will be more positive, too!

Talk to someone. You'll notice that we keep
suggesting that you to talk to someone about how
you feel. That's because we almost always feel
better when we can tell someone else how we feel.
Knowing that someone else understands how we
feel helps us begin to relax and feel better.

Ask for help. Usually kids feel discouraged when
they have trouble doing something. It can be very
discouraging when you try hard and you still are
not successful. So, what can you do? Ask for help!

Asking for help is different from asking someone to
do your work for you. Asking for help means getting
the information you need to succeed. You'll feel

more encouraged as soon as you know more about what to do.

Set goals that aren't too hard for you. Sometimes kids pick a goal that is way too hard. Then, when they can't reach their goal, they feel discouraged.

Instead of starting off with a huge goal, pick a smaller one. Once you have succeeded in accomplishing the smaller goal, you'll feel great.

Then set another small goal and work on it. Pretty soon you'll have lots of success and your discouraged feelings will be gone.

When You Feel LONELY

Everyone feels lonely sometimes. We feel lonely when we would like to be with someone, but there is no one around that we feel close to. It can feel lonely when you move to a new school before you make friends. It can feel lonely when your best friend has gone on vacation and there is no one to play with. And it can feel very lonely if other kids don't include you in their games on the playground or invite you to join them at lunch.

Here are some things that can help if you feel lonely.

Find someone to talk to. The easiest way to feel less lonely is to talk to someone else. Pick up the phone and call a friend or family member. They will be happy to hear from you! You could also email a friend to let them know how you're feeling.

Don't just sit there, do something! Here are some ideas you can try:

- Go outside and see if there are other kids around.
- Invite someone to come over and play.
- Ask your mom or dad to help you find group activities that you are interested in.
- Ask a family member to play a game or go for a walk with you.

Be a good friend to have a good friend. The best way to have a friend is to *be* a friend. You don't need to wait for others to be friendly to you. Start by being friendly toward others. That means:

- Smile and say "Hi."
- Be kind to others, especially to kids that may not have many friends.
- Try to help them feel better if they are upset or sad.
- Encourage other kids and tell them when they have done a good job at something.
- Make friends with kids that like to do the things you like to do.
- Remember to take turns and share.

When You Feel SCARED

It's no fun to feel scared. Sometimes kids feel scared of the dark, and are not comfortable being in their rooms alone at night. Other kids might be scared of bugs or spiders.

Use your good thinking to stop imagining scary things! When you are in bed at night and hear a little noise, does your imagination take over and scare you? Do you imagine that something very scary is about to happen?

Think about what else might be causing that noise to happen. Maybe it is just the wind or the TV downstairs or the furnace going on or off. Remind yourself that lots of things make noise and most of them aren't scary.

Use your imagination to make scary things into silly things. Instead of letting your imagination make you feel scared, use your imagination to help you feel safe! For example, when you feel scared of someone, imagine them wearing a ridiculous outfit. Pretty soon, you'll be giggling.

Or, if you're afraid of bugs, picture them with little roller skates on, not able to stand up. Instead of seeming scary, they'll look silly to you—this is what Ron Weasley does in *Harry Potter and the Prisoner of Azkaban.*

Whistle or sing a song if you feel scared. Music helps you change the way you feel. If you sing a happy, cheerful song, pretty soon you'll start feeling better and won't think so much about feeling scared.

Turn on a light if you feel scared in the dark. Lots of kids feel scared in the dark because they start to imagine scary things that are not real. One of the best solutions is to just turn on a light. Ask your mom or dad to put a night light in your room if you feel scared in the dark after you have gone to bed.

Snuggle with a pet or a stuffed animal if you feel scared because you are alone. It always helps to snuggle with a pet or a toy that makes you feel warm and safe.

Tell a grown-up if you are afraid that someone will hurt you. Don't ever let someone make you feel so scared that you are afraid to tell anyone. If you have been hurt, or if you are afraid that someone will hurt you, you should always tell a grown-up so that they can help you.

When You Feel WORRIED

Feeling worried is like feeling a little bit scared about things. Sometimes when children worry they think about something all of the time and their worry grows and grows.

Here are some things you can do to feel better when you are worried:

Tell a grown-up and get some help. Your parents, teacher, or another trusted grown-up can help you problem-solve and think of a way to calm your worries.

Talk to a friend about your worry. Sometimes when you talk to a friend they can tell you that they had the same worry before but now they feel better.

Prepare! If you are worried about something like a piano recital, or talking in front of your class, the best way to stop worrying is to prepare. Practice, practice, practice until you are sure you can do a good job.

Do something to relax. Go to your calm-down place, listen to peaceful music, or do a few minutes of meditation.

Get it over with! If you are worried about something that you are scared of, like getting a shot at the doctor's, the best thing is to just go ahead and do it. The longer you wait and think about it, the worse you will feel. Often, once you do the thing you worry about you'll see that it wasn't so big after all!

When You Feel EMBARRASSED

When you feel embarrassed, it can seem as if everyone is staring at you and you become very self-conscious.

Kids feel embarrassed when they think that they have messed up in some way in front of a lot of people.

Here are some things that can help you feel better if you feel embarrassed:

Change your thoughts to change your feelings. Instead of telling yourself that you were dumb to make a mistake, tell yourself that everyone makes mistakes.

Tell yourself that you don't have to be good at everything to feel good about yourself. Remind yourself that no one is good at everything. And you don't need to be good at everything to have friends.

Join in the joke. If you aren't worried about doing badly at something, and can even joke about it, then other kids will start laughing *with* you instead of laughing *at* you.

My Action Plan

Can you think of three feelings that you have that send you into your Upset Zone? Notice when you are having these feelings and rate them on a scale of one to ten, one being "not very much of this feeling" and ten being "in your Upset Zone." When you are experiencing a three or four on the scale, you might be heading into your Upset Zone. Use the Feel Good Tools in this chapter—or any other tools that work for you—to fill in the action plan below.

Here are the three feelings I would like to work on to stay out of my Upset Zone:

1._____

2._____

3._____

I am going to use these three tools to calm myself down so I can stay out of my Upset Zone:

1._____

2._____

3._____

Time for a Break!

Great job learning all those Feel Good Tools! You've earned a break. See if you can find the Feel Good Tools in the word search below.

WORD FIND !

```
N P Q T Z K F Y U O
E D M A R E I T S E
L B A C I N D J G K
I C F Y E I G N Q O
M P W V D O E D E J
S K Y T B R T J M X
M E M O R Y E T G D
O Q N D R K I A P S
S W O Y M O S U M E
P R E P A R E W K V
E Z F D G C B E T L
```

FIDGET   MEMORY
SMILE   DAY DREAM
JOKE   PREPARE

CHAPTER SIX

Problem-Solving So Upsets Come Less Often

WE have talked a lot about feelings that kids have when they have a problem. Now, it's time to talk about solving the problems that cause upset feelings.

How to Be a Champion Problem-Solver

Everyone has problems. Life is full of problems to solve. So, a good way to reduce upset feelings when problems happen is to turn yourself into a champion problem-solver! Here's how.

1. **Calm Down.** First, it's important to calm down so that you can think clearly. Go to your Action Plan on page 99 to remind yourself of your favorite ways to calm down.

2. **Focus on solutions instead of problems.** Instead of thinking, "Oh, no!" think, "OK, what can I do to fix this?"

3. **Think of many different solutions as you can.** If you can't think of any solutions, talk to other people who can give you some suggestions. Make a list of all of the solutions you can think of.

4. **Think about what might happen if you try each solution you think of.** If one of your solutions might lead to the outcome you want, it would be a good one to try first.

5. **Pick one of your solutions and try it.**

6. **Don't be discouraged if your first solution doesn't work.** Try to think like a detective looking for answers. If your solution doesn't work, try to figure out why it didn't work.

7. **Ask for help when you need it.** When you have a really big problem, ask for help from a parent or teacher.

8. **Don't give up—try again!** Then, change your solution so that it might work, or pick another solution and try that one.

How Megan Solved Her Problem

Megan felt lonely as she walked to school all alone. "Nobody likes me," she thought to herself. That morning, as she sat in class, she felt left out as the other kids talked to each other. She started crying and the teacher sent her down to the nurse's office. Megan had a problem—she felt like she had no friends. Here's how Megan used the problem-solving steps above to solve her problem and feel better:

1. **Calm down.** Megan lay down on the cot in the nurse's office and closed her eyes. Then she began to talk to the nurse, who was very kind, and Megan began to feel calmer. Talking to other people about your problem is often a good way to calm down.

2. **Focus on solutions instead of problems.** The nurse asked Megan if she could think of anything she could do differently to begin to make friends. The nurse reminded Megan to

think about solutions instead of just feeling sad about the problem.

3. **Think of many different solutions.** At first, Megan couldn't think of a solution, but the nurse gave her one idea. "How about asking someone in your class if she would like to walk to school with you in the morning? Does anyone live near you?" Then Megan started thinking of other possible solutions: "I could invite someone to play after school. I could share my cookies at lunchtime. I could bring my jump rope for recess and invite other girls to play with me."

4. **Consider the possible outcomes for each solution.** Megan thought that if she brought her jump rope for recess, lots of girls might play with her.

5. **Pick one and try it.** Megan decided to bring her jump rope to school the next day, but that didn't work because it was raining.

6. **Pick another one and try it.** So, Megan remembered not to give up and to try something else. She decided to look for Amy after school and ask her if she wanted to walk home together.

7. **Get help if it's a big problem.** Megan was a little shy and it was hard for her to make friends. She decided it would be good to get a little help with her problem. She decided to see the school

counselor. This time, Megan wasn't crying. She walked in to see the school counselor and said, "I want to find some solutions so that I can make friends at school." The counselor smiled and said, "Let's put on our thinking caps. Let's see. What are some things you could do? You had a good idea about your jump rope. Why don't you bring it back again tomorrow when it's not raining? And here's another idea. Why don't you practice just saying 'hello' and smiling when you see other kids in your class?"

Pretty soon they came up with lots of solutions to try.

8. **Don't give up, try again!** Megan tried bringing her jump rope again, and invited other girls to play with her at recess. Pretty soon Megan had two friends to play with after school and didn't feel sad, even on days she walked to school by herself.

Are you getting the hang of how problem-solving works? If there is a problem in your life that is causing you to be upset, try using these steps to solve the problem. Even just taking steps to solve the problem will help you feel better!

Time for a Break!

Megan lost her jump rope somewhere in her bedroom! *Can you find it?*

CHAPTER SEVEN

Special Projects With My Parents

CHANGING your behaviors isn't easy. It goes better when you work with someone who can remind you and encourage you. Working with your mom or dad can also help you get new ideas. For example, when you are trying to problem-solve, your mom or dad might be able to think of a way to solve your problem that you haven't thought of.

Remember to focus on things that *you* can change. You might want everyone at school to get along, or for your teacher to be nicer to you, but that isn't really something under your control. However, *you* are in charge of your behavior!

Don't try to change everything at once. Pick one area and work on that until you develop new habits. Then you can move on to a new area until pretty soon you feel calmer and better most of the time.

Working Together on Changes

When you decide on something you want to change, your mom or dad can help you and support you in lots of ways. They can help you brainstorm ways to make changes, remind you, and—best of all—reward you when you stick to your goal.

For example, let's say that you have decided to work on recognizing the warning signs that you are moving toward your Upset Zone.

Your mom or dad can help you make a chart of your warning signs so that you can pay better attention to them when they happen. Maybe your teacher will let you tape it to your desk in school, too.

Here's an example of a warning signs list that you might make with your mom or dad.

MY WARNING SIGNS:

⦿ I AM TIRED AFTER A LONG DAY.

⦿ I AM HUNGRY BEFORE DINNER.

⦿ I AM FRUSTRATED WHEN DOING MY HOMEWORK.

Then, they can help you come up with ways to avoid these warning signs:

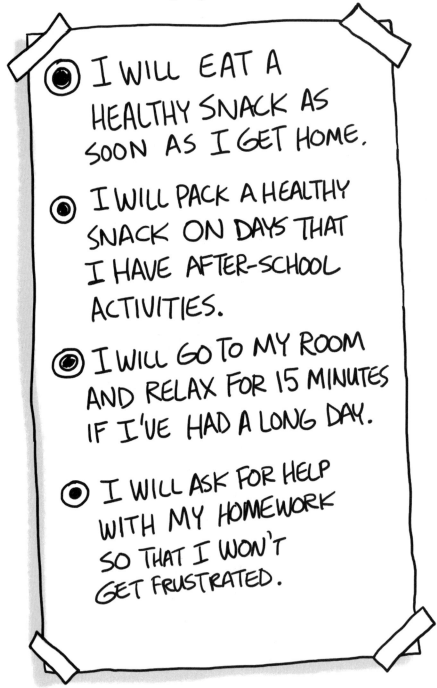

- I WILL EAT A HEALTHY SNACK AS SOON AS I GET HOME.

- I WILL PACK A HEALTHY SNACK ON DAYS THAT I HAVE AFTER-SCHOOL ACTIVITIES.

- I WILL GO TO MY ROOM AND RELAX FOR 15 MINUTES IF I'VE HAD A LONG DAY.

- I WILL ASK FOR HELP WITH MY HOMEWORK SO THAT I WON'T GET FRUSTRATED.

Whatever project you pick to work on, your mom or dad can help by finding a way to remind you. Your mom and dad can also reward you when you make progress. You can work together to make a list of small rewards that you can earn every day that you succeed with your new habit.

Here are some small daily rewards that other families have chosen:

- Playing a board game with a parent
- Playing ball for 15 minutes with a parent
- Eliminating a daily chore
- Playing a computer game for 15 minutes with a parent
- 20 minutes of a favorite activity after homework is done
- Inviting a friend over to play after school
- Baking cookies

You can also make a list of bigger rewards with your mom or dad. These bigger rewards are things that you can earn by earning small rewards for a certain number of times. Here is a list of bigger rewards that other families have chosen:

- Ordering a home-delivered pizza
- Inviting a friend to spend the night
- Having movie night at home with popcorn and favorite snacks
- Staying up a half-hour late on a weekend night

Can you and your parents think of other small rewards and bigger rewards to add to your reward list?

Step-by-Step Plan for Making Changes

1. Make a list called "Things I want to Change." A good place to start is to look back to your list, "Ways to Deal With My Warning Signs," on page 56. You might want to pick something on this list to work on. For example, if being tired is one of your warning signs, you could work on getting to bed on time each night. You could also refer to your action plan on page 99, and work on using the tools that help you feel better when you're heading into your Upset Zone.

2. Go to this list and pick something you want to work on with your mom or dad.

3. Only pick one thing—don't try to do too much at one time.

4. Start with something easier so that you can be successful.

5. Decide on a reward with your mom or dad—something small that you can look forward to each day that you succeed with your new habit. You could also pick one bigger reward for when you've stuck to your plan for a certain amount of time.

6. Track your progress. You can use the progress chart on page 117, or come up with a different one with your parents.

7. Don't try to be perfect. Change is hard. Just try each day and keep a record of your success.

8. Think about how much better things will be when you feel calmer most of the time.

9. Give yourself positive messages, just like the Little Engine That Could!

Progress Chart

Wow! Congratulations! You've finished the book.

You have learned a lot of things about feelings. There are many kinds of feelings aren't there? It is really important to learn about your own feelings and about how to stay out of your Upset Zone.

Make a progress chart of the new habit you want to work on.

Fill it out each day with your mom or dad.

Remember, pay attention to improving. Don't try to be perfect. If you slip up, think of a solution to fix the slip-up and give yourself credit for that!

Talk to your mom or dad about your progress and ask their advice when you have trouble with your new habit.

Celebrate your progress and problem-solve when you get off-track.

You can make a photocopy of the chart of page 117 and tape it where you will see it every day to help remind you of what to do to calm down and stay cool.

Progress Chart

Week number____

I'm working on _____

_____

How am I doing?

	Off Track	Getting Better	Super Job!
Day 1	☐	☐	☐
Day 2	☐	☐	☐
Day 3	☐	☐	☐
Day 4	☐	☐	☐
Day 5	☐	☐	☐
Day 6	☐	☐	☐
Day 7	☐	☐	☐

Problem-solving

When I'm trying to _____

_____ but I get off track:

What's the problem? _____

_____

What are some things I can do to try to solve the problem?

1. _____

2. _____

3. _____

Reward Yourself!

Time to reward yourself for all your hard work!

Decode the words below. Then fill in the blanks to reveal a secret message!

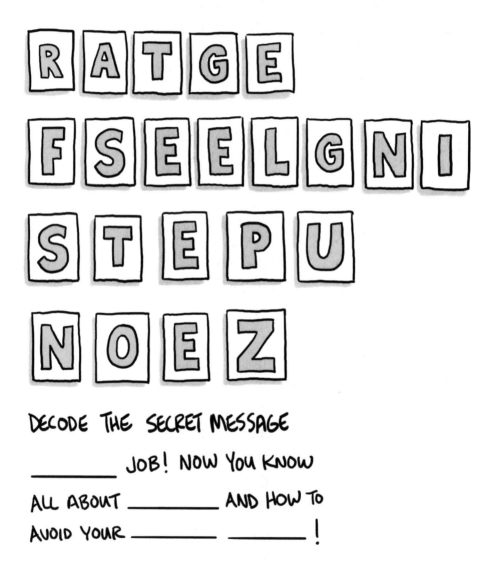

DECODE THE SECRET MESSAGE

_____ JOB! NOW YOU KNOW

ALL ABOUT _____ AND HOW TO

AVOID YOUR _____ _____ !

Note to Parents

THE more you can learn about effective behavior management for your child, the more helpful this book will be. Below, you will find a list of ways to reward your child, ways to build a more positive relationship with your child, and organizations that may be helpful as you and your child work to gain better control over upset feelings.

It can also be helpful to work on some of these ideas yourself, together with your child. Fill out your own Action Plan and Progress Chart.

Remember:

- Small, immediate rewards are more effective than bigger rewards that take longer to reach.
- A combination of small immediate rewards and points toward a bigger reward can be even more effective.
- Be VERY clear about how your child earns rewards and points—write it down so that there is no misunderstanding.
- Reward improvement, not perfection!
- Set reachable goals with your child. If you set a goal that is too hard to reach you will only discourage yourself and your child. Even a *huge* reward won't help your child reach a goal that is too big a change. Take change step by step and celebrate every small sign of improvement.

- Don't try to change too many things at once. Most of us can only work on two or three things at a time.
- Kids with AD/HD do better if they have visual reminders. Try making a copy of each of the lists in this book and posting them in their room or on the refrigerator to help them remember.
- Try to make the rewards happen when and where the behavior happens.
- Get the support that you need as a parent to be calm, consistent, and encouraging as you work with your child to develop new habits.
- Remember, changing is hard work. Don't emphasize set-backs. Instead, focus on improvements, however small. For example, if your child has a huge upset, but comes back to apologize, focus on the apology. Congratulate your child for calming down and coming back to apologize. Encourage them and tell them that you can see they are doing better. Don't over-focus on the upset. Help your child problem-solve to see if you can find a way to avoid an upset next time.

Reward Your Child

The most rewarding thing that you can offer your child is positive, one-on-one time. Don't get caught up in giving your child too many sweets or costly items. There are many very rewarding things you can do that are healthy for your child and won't break the family budget. For example:

- Play a card game or board game with your child.
- Give permission to have a play date.
- Do a cooking project together.
- Play a computer game with your child.
- Watch a DVD together.
- Make popcorn necklaces with your child—then eat them!
- Allow your child to watch a half-hour of TV after homework is done.
- Get a "free pass" from doing a chore.
- Order a pizza on Friday night if your child has had a good week.
- Let your child stay up an hour later on a weekend night.
- Let your child have a sleep-over as a reward for a good week.
- Go bike-riding with your child.
- Play catch with your child.
- Read your child an extra story at bedtime.
- Give your child a special back-rub at bedtime.

Make a Clear Plan and Write It Down

Be very clear about what your child needs to do to earn a specific reward. The last thing you want to do is to create an upset because there was a misunderstanding about how she can earn a reward.

Make it easy to earn rewards. The more your child succeeds, the harder she will try. For example, if evening upsets are very regular at your house, start by rewarding a calm down and apology following the upset. Don't expect your child to suddenly stop getting upset. Reward shorter periods of upset. Look for small improvements and notice them, encourage them, and reward them.

You can also give them opportunities to practice calming skills when they are not upset and reward them for doing so.

In that way they can learn to use the skills and then it will be easier to use them when they need them.

Encourage Your Child

Be generous with your encouragement. Your child will thrive on positive feedback, such as:

- Hugs
- Pats
- Smiles
- "Way to go!"
- "Great job!"
- "I know how hard you are trying."
- "I'm proud of you."
- "That's awesome!"
- "High–five!"
- "Nice work!"

Plan Special Time With Your Child

"Special time" is different from reward time. Research shows that as little as five minutes each day of special time can make a huge positive difference in your relationship with your child.

Special time is a time for you to just sit with your child as he or she sits and plays. Creative toys that don't have rules or points make the best special time activities—dolls, puppets, Legos, or other construction toys work well.

During special time your role is to:

- Reflect: "You're building a tower!"
- Praise the child's activity: "What a great tower you're building!"
- Describe: "Oh, now you're building a bridge to the tower."
- Enjoy: Smile and show your child how much you enjoy his or her company during this special time.

During special time, don't criticize, instruct, question, or give advice. This is a time for your child to bask in your undivided attention while doing an activity in which there is no right or wrong.

Think of this special time as a "medicine" that your child needs every day. On days when there has been more conflict, special time is even more important.

Find the Resources That Your Child Needs

If your child struggles with emotional control, look for as much support as you can find. Look for parent support groups in your area. Join organizations that advocate for issues that your child may struggle with.

Work closely with your child's teacher and school counselor to problem-solve and try to reduce situations at school that may fuel frequent upsets. Advocate for your child if you believe that he is the victim of bullying at school.

Often, upsets are the result of chronic frustrations related to learning or attentional problems. Be sure that your child has received a comprehensive assessment so that all issues are being addressed.

Below, you'll find a list of resources that may be helpful to you as you look for supports for yourself and your child.

Some children benefit from having therapy to help them learn coping skills to manage their feelings.

Websites for Finding a Child or Family Therapist

American Psychological Association: www.apa.org

National Register of Health Service Psychologists: www.findapsychologist.org

Other Helpful Websites

Children and Adults with Attention-Deficit/Hyperactivity Disorder (CHADD): www.chadd.org

Center for Collaborative Problem Solving: www.ccps.info

Circle of Security: http://circleofsecurity.net

LD Online: www.ldonline.org

National Library of Medicine, Medline Plus: http://www.nlm.nih.gov/medlineplus

Research Based Parenting: http://www.alankazdin.com

Social Thinking: www.socialthinking.com

Meditation Resources

CDs

Airy Melody. (2008). *Rainbows and sunshine* [CD]. Upton, MA: Airy Melody Music, LLC.

Kabat-Zinn, J. (2007). *Mindfulness for beginners* [CD]. Boulder, CO: Sounds True, Inc.

Lite, L. (2005). *Indigo ocean dreams* [CD]. Marietta, GA: Stress Free Kids.

Lite, L. (2006). *Indigo dreams: Garden of wellness* [CD]. Marietta, GA: Stress Free Kids.

Lite, L. (2010). *Indigo dreams* [CD]. Marietta, GA: Stress Free Kids.

Lite, L. (2010). *Indigo dreams: Rainforest relaxation* [CD]. Marietta, GA; Stress Free Kids.

Books

Fontana, D., & Slack, I. *Teaching meditation to children: The practical guide to the use and benefits of meditation techniques.* London, England: Watkins.

Garth, M. (1991). *Starbright: Meditations for children.* New York, NY: HarperOne.

Garth, M. (1993). *Moonbeam: A book of meditations for children.* New York, NY: HarperOne.

Garth, M. (1997). *Earthlight: New meditations for children.* New York, NY: HarperOne.

Holitzka, K. (2000). *Power mandalas.* New York, NY: Sterling Publishing Co., Inc.

MacLean, K. L. (2004). *Peaceful piggy meditation.* Morton Grove, IL: Albert Whitman & Company.

Vallely, S. W. (2008). *Sensational meditation for children: Child-friendly meditation techniques based on the five senses.* Asheville, NC: Satya International, Inc.

Books for Parents:

Degangi, G., & Kendall, A. (2008). *Effective parenting for the hard-to-manage child: A skills-based book.* New York: Routledge Taylor and Francis Group.

Greene, R. (2010). *The explosive child: A new approach for understanding and parenting easily frustrated, chronically inflexible children.* New York: Harper Collins Publishers.

Hamil, S. (2008). *My feeling better workbook: Help for kids who are sad and depressed.* Oakland, CA: New Harbinger Publications.

Harvey, P., & Penzo, J. (2009). *Parenting a child who has intense emotions: Dialectical behavior therapy skills to help your child regulate emotional outbursts and aggressive behaviors.* Oakland, CA: New Harbinger Publications, Inc.

Kazdin, A. (2009). *The Kazdin method for parenting the defiant child.* New York, NY: Mariner Books.

Kuypers, L. (2011). *The zones of regulation: A curriculum designed to foster self-regulation and emotional control.* San Jose, CA: Think Social Publishing, Inc.

Schab, L. (2009). *Cool, calm, confident: A workbook to help kids learn assertiveness skills.* Oakland, CA: New Harbinger Publications.

Shapiro, L., & Sprague, R. (2009). *The relaxation and stress reduction workbook for kids: Help for children to cope with stress, anxiety and transitions.* Oakland, CA: New Harbinger Publications.

Stallard, P. (2002). *Think good—feel good: A cognitive behavior therapy workbook for children and young people.* Hoboken, NJ: John Wiley & Sons, Ltd.

Books for Kids:

Craver, M. M. (2012). *Chillax! How Ernie learns to chill out, relax, and take charge of his anger.* Washington, DC: Magination Press.

Gordon, J. (2012). *The energy bus for kids: A story about staying positive and overcoming challenges.* Hoboken, NJ: John Wiley & Sons, Inc.

Huebner, D. (2005). *What to do when you worry too much: A kid's guide to overcoming anxiety.* Washington, DC: Magination Press.

Huebner, D. (2007). *What to do when you grumble too much: A kid's guide to overcoming negativity.* Washington, DC: Magination Press.

Huebner, D. (2007). *What to do when your temper flares: A kid's guide to overcoming problems with anger.* Washington, DC: Magination Press.

Huebner, D. (2008). *What to do when you dread your bed: A kid's guide to overcoming problems with sleep.* Washington, DC: Magination Press.

Kraus, J. (2013). *Get ready for Jetty! My journal about AD/HD and me.* Washington, DC: Magination Press.

Lamia, M. C. (2013). *Emotions: Making sense of your feelings.* Washington, DC: Magination Press.

Lamia, M. C. (2011). *Understanding myself: A kid's guide to intense emotions and strong feelings.* Washington, DC: Magination Press.

Madison, L. (2002). *The feelings book: The care and keeping of your emotions.* Middleton, WI: American Girl Publishing, Inc.

Madison, L. (2005). *The feelings book journal.* Middleton, WI: American Girl Publishing, Inc.

Mangan, T. (2012). *How to feel good: 20 things teens can do.* Washington, DC: Magination Press.

Nadeau, K. G., & Dixon, E. B. (2005). *Learning to slow down and pay attention: A book for kids about AD/HD* (3rd ed.). Washington, DC: Magination Press.

Quinn, P. O. (2009). *Attention, girls! A guide to learn all about your AD/HD.* Washington, DC: Magination Press.

Quinn, P. O., & Stern, J. (2012). *Putting on the brakes: Understanding and taking control of your ADD or AD/HD* (3rd ed.). Washington, DC: Magination Press.

About the Authors

Judith M. Glasser, PhD, is a clinical psychologist who has worked with children and their families for over 30 years. She specializes in the assessment and treatment of AD/HD in children. For many years Dr. Glasser has been interested in the different kinds of difficulties children experience when they have AD/HD. Many of the children she works with struggle with learning how to handle their feelings; this book is for them.

Kathleen Nadeau, PhD, is a clinical psychologist who has specialized in working with kids and adults with ADHD for many years. She is the founder and director of the Chesapeake ADHD Center in Silver Spring, MD, and the author of many books on ADHD for kids, teens, adults, and professionals. Dr. Nadeau is a frequent lecturer on topics related to ADHD, both in the United States and abroad.

About the Illustrator

Charles Beyl creates humorous illustrations for books, magazines, and newspapers from his studio high atop a nineteenth-century Pennsylvania farm house.

About Magination Press

Magination Press is an imprint of the American Psychological Association, the largest scientific and professional organization representing psychologists in the United States and the largest association of psychologists worldwide.